The
Frankenstein
Steps
& Other Adventures

The Frankenstein Steps
& Other Adventures

by Stephen Bowkett

Illustrated by Jamie Egerton
Cover design by Sandi Patterson

NEP
PO Box 635
Stafford
ST16 1BF

First published 2001
© Stephen Bowkett 2001

ISBN – 185539 086 8

Illustrations by Jamie Egerton
Cover illustration by Sandi Patterson
Edited by Anne Oppenheimer
Design by Neil Hawkins

Printed in Great Britain by
MPG Books Ltd., Bodmin, Cornwall

Acknowledgements

Thanks to Sandi Patterson and Jamie Egerton for great visuals, to Anne Oppenheimer for such effective editing (as usual) and to all members of the Double Dare Gang wherever you may be.

Stephen Bowkett
July 2001

You can read more about the Double Dare Gang in:
The Allotment Ghost & Other Adventures

This book is part of an educational package called *ALPS StoryMaker*, which uses fiction as a resource for Accelerated Learning.

For further details go to www.sbowkett.freeserve.co.uk or contact Network Educational Press on 01785 225515 or via www.networkpress.co.uk

The Double Dare Gang

Code of Honour

- LIVE TO DARE - DARE TO LIVE!
- HONOUR THE DOUBLE DARE GANG!
- HONOUR YOUR FELLOW DOUBLE-DARERS.
- SHOW RESPECT - HURT NO-ONE.
- THE WORLD IS THE QUESTION - YOUR LIFE IS THE ANSWER.
- THE GREAT ADVENTURE HAS BEGUN.

We are defined by our choices

DDG Forever!!

Contents

The Frankenstein Steps

I tried hard not to think about the afternoon growing darker outside. We had been invited up to Nige's house so his mum could meet 'all these new friends' she'd heard so much about. That really embarrassed Nigel, because now that Anna Williams was one of the Double Darers, she had to come too.

Mrs Lloyd did us baked potatoes with cheese and beans, and a trifle for afters. And there was plenty of cola or lemonade, whichever you preferred. As we ate, she looked at us all very carefully, though with a pleasant, friendly smile on her face.

"I think you've got to know some very nice people, Nigel," she told him after the meal, beaming at each of us. She glanced at me in particular. "Your mother works at the post office, doesn't she, on Patrick Street?"

I nodded. "But only on Friday afternoons and Saturdays, and to cover in the holidays when other people are off..."

"I knew your mum well, some years ago. We were both dinner ladies down at the Bowden school."

Mum had told me about her school dinner days; though I was in the infants then, and didn't really remember it. I was surprised that Mrs Lloyd had done such an ordinary job as well, because although Nige was a real scruff-bag, the family lived in a big house at the top of town, on Clack Hill. They must have been quite well off, I guessed.

I didn't quite know what to say in reply to Mrs Lloyd's comment; and the others were going towards the door and I didn't want to be left behind.

Mrs Lloyd beamed at me briefly.

"You go along with your pals – the Double Dare Gang, isn't it?"

I nodded.

She chuckled. "But pop in to see me before you go home, Stephen. I'll write a note for your mother, and you can take it back for me."

"All right Mrs Lloyd. Thanks... See you later."

* * *

It was later, and we'd been talking about ghosts. Halloween and Bonfire Night were not far away, and the evenings had a chill about them now, and that early darkness which turned your thoughts towards the shadows.

Nige had told a good story about a local ghost that was supposed to walk around the town with its head under its arm. Kev told us about the Halloween Man, who had a hollowed-out pumpkin for a head.

Anthony told a story about a phantom that haunted the railway, and I made up a load of stuff about the monster plesiosaur that haunted the Lime Pools.

Halfway through Kevin's story, Nige had turned on the lamp he'd brought from his room. We had electric power in the shed but the lamp had just a little bulb and was battery powered, and gave out this really faint and spooky light.

"It's your turn now, Anna..." Nige's grin looked wicked in the dimness. He hadn't quite forgiven Anna yet for passing the bravery test on the Rope Swing – nor for giving him a big sloppy kiss in front of his mates. Maybe he thought he could embarrass her now, if she didn't have a story to tell...

"Well," she said, giving Nige a sideways glance. "There is this thing that happened to my brother, Dave... But I think it's too scary for you to hear."

"Ha!" Neil gave a scornful hoot. He hadn't forgiven Anna either, for toppling him over when she tigged him: and because a couple of us had started calling him a beached whale.

"Bet you couldn't scare us if you tried." Neil folded his arms and glared at Anna challengingly.

"You're probably right," she said, leaning back into the shadows.

"Oh, go on Anna, tell us what happened to Dave," I said. "I dare you..."

She leaned forward again into the light and her face was full of mischief. I reckoned I was beginning to understand more about Anna Williams: about how she liked to play games, and win...

"It happened a couple of years ago," Anna began, as we settled ourselves to listen. "Dave is ten years older than me, and he was going to college at the time, in Spring Falls. The summer holidays came along, and Dave decided to take a break – just to get away from it all and have some peace and quiet. Normally he found a summer job, but this time he just wanted to relax.

"Because he didn't have much money, he

thought he'd go camping. He packed up a haversack, and hitched a lift all the way up the motorway to Scotland. Then he hitched another lift to Dumfries, and another one into the Galloway hills..."

"I been to Dumfries," Neil proclaimed.

"Shut up and let her tell it," Nige grumbled at him irritably.

"The journey had taken all day, and it was late in the afternoon when Dave found himself in the middle of nowhere. The sun had set beyond the hills, and a chilly wind was blowing in off the sea. Dave noticed that some black rainclouds were coming over. Soon it would be pouring, and he didn't want to get caught out in it.

"The trouble was, he couldn't see a light shining anywhere. There didn't seem to be even a farmhouse in sight. He hadn't brought a tent: all he had was a sleeping bag.

"Dave looked around, starting to get a bit worried

by now. Then, in the gloom, he noticed the shadowy shape of what looked like a house and a barn, down in the glen. No lights were showing there, but at least it was shelter. He left the road and followed the rough track, arriving at the farmhouse just as the rain began.

"Dave was disappointed to find that the house itself was all boarded up and abandoned. The door was padlocked. It looked as though the place had been empty for a long time. But attached to the house was a large barn, and although the big double doors were also locked, a small hatchway door cut into them could be opened. Dave went inside just as the downpour really started!

"Inside the barn it was very dark, and it took a couple of minutes for Dave's eyes to adjust. He began to make out shapes in the shadows, and realised the place was piled up with furniture; just kind of dumped in there, as though it had been removed from the house and then left.

"Dave unslung his haversack and rolled out his

sleeping bag. He was patting it flat – when a sudden movement startled him.

"A small child came round from behind the piles of furniture – a young girl of about eight or nine. Dave's heart gave a great thump of shock, but then he looked concerned... Because this little girl seemed very thin and very pale, and she had these big, dark, staring, soulful eyes. The weirdest thing, though, was that she was dressed in an old-fashioned nightgown that went down to her ankles and was buttoned up at the chin. It had a lacy collar.

"Dave stood up slowly and stared at the silent girl, who simply gazed back at him. She seemed so lost and alone. He felt sorry for her.

"Finally, to break the silence, he said, 'Hello, little girl. What's your name? Mine's Dave'."

"For a few moments the girl didn't reply, then her mouth opened and she said, in a sort of echoing whisper, 'I haven't got a name...'

"Dave frowned. He didn't know quite what to do.

'Um, well look, it's raining quite heavily now. But when it stops, I'll take you home, OK?'

"And the little girl said, 'But I haven't got a home...'

"Dave was starting to worry now, because there seemed to be something very strange about this child. Although the rain had cooled the air down and it was chilly in the barn, she didn't seem to be shivering: she didn't seem to notice the cold at all.

" 'Look,' Dave said, 'your parents are going to be worried about you...'

"'But I haven't got any parents,' the child told him in that odd, distant voice. He thought then she must be ill; confused maybe, or escaped from somewhere.

"Outside, the wind lifted and lashed the raindrops against the west-facing wall of the barn. Dave took off his jacket.

"'Little girl,' he said, 'why don't you wear this jacket? It'll keep you warm. I don't want you getting the flu or anything, because it could go down on to your chest – and that's bad for your heart...'

"And the pale child looked up at Dave, as though seeing him for the first time. She smiled a ghastly red smile, and she answered, 'But I haven't got a heart.' She pulled her nightdress aside to show the skeleton bones beneath. 'I've got a Rrrraaaggghhh!' "

Anna leaped up and dived towards us.

Neil let out a scream and fell over backwards. All of us jumped, Kev's flailing arm knocking over the little lamp, which flew into the corner and dropped out of sight.

The shed was plunged into darkness and confusion. And then, as we got over the shock, Nige and then Bri, Anthony, me and Kev began to laugh. We laughed until we cried. And then we laughed some more, helplessly, as Neil's small voice piped up.

"Hey everybody, I've just done a botty burp..."

* * *

No-one could be in any doubt after that – Anna Williams was a true and worthy member of the DDG. Her story had put us in the mood for more, but of course, nobody could follow it. And in any case, it was getting late and we would be expected back at our homes.

We made plans to meet again at the weekend, then Nige flung open the door of the garden shed to let in the night...

Going out into the garden was not like stepping back into the real world. The wind had got up, and purplish-grey clouds were moving quickly overhead. It was still light enough to see, but in twenty minutes the last of the daylight would be gone. Worse than that, Anna's story still haunted us: I could see the little girl with no heart suddenly flying towards Anna's brother, her mouth splitting open wider, and huge teeth suddenly appearing. And then... And then...

We had followed Nige down the side of the house. As we reached the front path, a hand came out and grabbed me by the shoulder.

"Agh! Mummy!"

I struggled to escape, until I realised it was Mrs Lloyd holding something out towards me.

"Stephen, you nearly forgot, didn't you?"

The other kids were giggling as my mouth opened and closed like a goldfish.

"The letter I wanted you to take to your mother... It'll save me the cost of a stamp."

"Oh, yes..." I took the envelope and stuffed it in the back pocket of my jeans.

"Thanks, Mrs Lloyd..."

"It'll be nice to see your mum again. Give her my regards, won't you?"

"Yes, I will," I said, as she went inside, leaving us standing by the porch.

"Right then," Neil said, much too chirpily. "I'll be off." He hung around to see if anyone was going to offer to go with him – but nobody did, and he made his way cautiously to the front gate, checking to make sure no monsters were lurking in the street.

"Hey Neil!" Nige called, as Neil started scuttling home. "Watch out you don't get grabbed by the ghoulies!"

I laughed with everyone else at the tired old joke, but I had to walk home too, and all of a sudden the idea didn't appeal to me so much.

Anna must have seen the look on my face by the light of the porch. She smiled, and her eyes were all twinkly.

"Don't worry Steve, I'll walk up the street with you..."

Nige's ears pricked up.

"Make sure you hold hands," he said nastily. Beside him, Brian guffawed.

"Um, it's OK, Anna, thanks, but – "

"What I mean," she replied, "is that I need somebody to walk me home – well, part of the way at least."

"What a hero you are, Steve," Kev chortled. "You can't leave the girl to walk home alone now, can you?"

"Oh, all right then," I said, wondering if Anna was trying to spare my embarrassment, or was still playing her games.

I jammed my hands in my pockets and strode off down the path, hooking open the front gate with my foot, and not caring if it swung shut as Anna hurried along to catch up with me.

Although I thought she was OK – I quite liked her in fact – I didn't particularly want to talk to her or anything. Neil and Anthony were not that far behind us, and I was scared they'd get the wrong idea.

"Where do you live?" Anna asked just then. I sighed, realising I couldn't get out of the dilemma.

"Corner of Cross Street and Maple Road," I answered quietly; so that if Neil and Anthony heard Anna talking, they'd think I hadn't bothered to reply.

"I live on the new estate," she added, "Lazy Acres.

Mum and Dad have called our house 'The Shambles'!"

She smiled, and I smiled back at her. "Our house isn't called the shambles – it is a shambles..."

"Your quickest way home is down the steps that come out close by the railway station..."

"Yeah, you're right..."

"My quickest route is to carry on to the main road, then down Bowden Hill to the estate," Anna said. I hoped she wasn't going to suggest that I see her to her door. Apart from being totally uncool, it would add twenty minutes to my journey, by which time Mum would be going spare.

So I didn't offer, and we walked along for a while in silence.

"You know what they call those steps, don't you?"

"What steps?"

"The ones down to the railway station..." Anna pointed to the alley where the steps began. "The

Frankenstein Steps, that's what they're called."

"I've never heard that."

She shrugged lightly and stared ahead. "Maybe people don't talk about it much these days. But Dave, that's my older brother, you remember, he said that years ago a strange figure used to haunt Bowden Hill. No-one ever knew why. A few times it was seen on the railway station – always on the northbound platform, Dave said. And occasionally people spotted it right on the top of Bowden Hill... There used to be a gallows up there, you know. Maybe that's got something to do with it. But most often, the ghostly figure was reported on the steps... And because of the way the phantom walked, kind of awkwardly, with its arms stretched out in front, the place became known as the Frankenstein Steps...

"It's probably all nonsense," Anna concluded, looking at me innocently. "But you know people love to pretend these scary stories actually happened!"

"Huh, yeah, I know," I said. I glanced back to

catch sight of Neil and Anthony, but then remembered they turned off down Meadowdale Way to get home. We came to the alley and Anna stopped.

"Look, Steve," she said seriously, "there's no need for you to walk with me any more. I'll be all right. It's not far from here anyway, and there're plenty of streetlights."

"Oh, well, if you're sure..."

"I'm sure... So long, then. I'll see you at the weekend."

"Bye, Anna," I said, as she turned and walked confidently away up the street. I watched until she turned the corner of Elm Drive and disappeared.

And then I was alone.

"Just a load of nonsense," I told myself. "'Frankenstein Steps' – huh! She's just winding me up..."

I walked through the alley between the houses,

and the wind caught me as I reached the top of the steps, which wound down the hill like a broad ribbon to the distant lights of the railway station below.

It seemed like a million miles away.

The chilly gust had made my eyes water. I rubbed at them, then scanned the steps carefully for any sign of someone – of something – lurking there. Of course there was nobody; though it would have been nice if a train had just stopped at the station, and a load of people coming home from work had been making their way up towards me.

I had never counted the steps, but I reckoned there were about a hundred and fifty of them. There was a streetlight at the top (I was standing right under it), one in the middle, and one at the bottom...

With great stretches of darkness in between.

Even though I kept telling myself that Anna had just been trying to scare me, I felt all fluttery inside. And I didn't want to begin the journey down, because I thought that if I began to panic, I'd just run faster and faster – until I couldn't stop – and the wind would whirl me up – right into the arms of the man who'd been hanged on the Bowden Hill gallows - and then we'd both haunt the Frankenstein Steps forever!

In the town, I heard the church clock striking the hour. Six o'clock. I knew that Mum would be worrying – so I took a deep breath and started on my way.

As the brightness of the streetlight faded and the shadows gathered round, thoughts of ghosts and monsters and things that lived in darkness in the ground began growing in my head. I imagined the girl who had no heart, that poor lost little soul; and the Halloween Man with a pumpkin for a head; and the railway phantom... I even pictured my plesiosaur rising up from the green depths of the Lime Pools, breaking surface and letting out a mournful, bellowing howl...

I began counting the steps out loud, to calm myself down.

"One... two... three... four..." Then I counted seconds to keep myself busier. "Five-one-forty... Six-one-forty... Seven-one-forty..."

After a couple of minutes I reached the safety of the middle streetlight; a pool of comfort where I could rest for a moment or two.

The night was huge on either side of me. I looked down to the bottom of the steps. They were deserted. I looked back up to the top –

And a figure was running down after me, his arms held out in front.

A horrible tight feeling like a plum-stone got caught in my throat. My face went very hot, but the rest of my body turned cold: so cold that I seemed to be frozen. I thought, if I faint now he'll get me; he'll get his rotten dead hands on my neck!

I thought I was going to scream, but what came out was a silly little whimper.

To run away, I had to turn my back on the thing that was following me. It didn't feel as though I was

properly in my body at all. It was like working a clumsy puppet, not knowing which strings to pull to make the legs move.

Even so, I rattled down the steps, faster and faster, and kept whispering, "Don't get me – please – don't get me – please – don't get me ... please."

The monster called out in a loud, hollow voice.

"Little boy! Little boy!"

"He knows I'm here – he knows I'm here – and he's catching me, oh God, he's catching me!"

"Little boy! Stop!"

Instead of thinking about him – about It – I decided to pretend I was a champion sprinter. The light at the end of the steps was the winning line. And because I was the best in the world, no-one and nothing could catch me!

But I was moving as quickly as I could, right on the edge where my running might go out of control. I paced it, keeping it steady, leaping the steps two at a time. I was flying along, leaving the hanged man far behind, farther and farther behind, getting smaller and smaller...

Ten steps to go. I took two in a great flying stride –another two – another two –

I didn't even see where the lip of the next step had crumbled. But I felt it as my foot caught the uneven edge, twisted sideways and flung me to the ground.

I hit the stone with a clunk of elbows and knees, suddenly sick with the white-hot pain of my wrenched ankle. It hurt so much I couldn't think about the monster until I heard him clumping closer.

I tried desperately to scramble away, but the shadow fell over me and strong hands turned me around.

I thought – so this is what happens to little kids who stay out too late. They haunt the night with the ghost of the Frankenstein Steps. I got ready to die.

"Hey, are you all right?"

It was a man's voice, concerned but friendly at the same time. He was holding something out to me. And behind the outstretched hand was a human face, a normal face. He had a moustache.

"You dropped this envelope... Sorry if I startled you, son."

"It's OK mister," I managed to say. And then, checking that no-one else from the Double Dare Gang was anywhere near, I allowed myself to burst into tears.

Wise Guy

"**R**ight!" Mr Jesson, the Scout Master, bellowed through his electronic megaphone.

"Will you please bring your bits and pieces over to the gap in the fence, and the helpers will take it from there... Thanks for your efforts, boys and girls, ladies and gentlemen. And don't forget, we've still got two days to make this the best bonfire the town has ever seen!"

Mr Jesson signed off with a shriek of feedback and an amplified click. Then he began to direct the kids from the First Kenniston Scout Group, pointing this way and that in an effort to make sure the bonfire was piled up equally on every side. It was already at least twenty feet tall: a huge wigwam of sticks, planks and boxes built around an old wardrobe that somebody's dad had donated. Several doors stuck out at odd angles from the mass; and about three quarters of the way up was a small armchair, tilted upwards, on which the guy was to sit...

Which particular guy it was to be had not been decided. Mr Jesson had organised a 'Guy of the Year' competition. Anybody could enter. The idea was that you built your guy, went round doing penny-for-the-guy on Friday and Saturday night, then on Sunday afternoon – November Fifth – the judging took place. The winning team would get free entry to the bonfire party, plus a token for free hot-dogs and cola.

"Sounds like a good deal," Nige said as he handed over two carrier bags filled with egg cartons.

Bri nodded enthusiastically. "I like the idea of the

free hot-dogs, Nige."

"Yeah – and that's a token for each member of the team, not one between the lot of us."

"Well – " Kevin dumped a pile of newspapers over the picket fence surrounding the bonfire. "Are we going to enter, or what?"

"I'm game," I said. "My Dad was going through some stuff in the attic the other day. He brought down a load of old clothes from the 'Seventies – I mean, weird! Bright coloured shirts that look as though they're all wrinkled up – "

"It's called seersucker," Anna said. "The material, I mean. It used to be all the rage."

"It'd put me in a rage if I had to wear it... And his trousers, you should see the size of the flares!"

"I think we're on to something." Nige was rubbing his chin thoughtfully. "If we really made the guy look like it came from the 'Seventies, I mean, lots of grownups were young then. It'll be a trip down memory lane. What's it called? Nostalgia. It'll be nostalgia for them. They're bound to give us lots of money..."

"If the guy's good enough," Kev said. "Hey, Anna, you're a girl – you could do all the sewing and stuff!"

"You mean, while you're resting up in bed with a fat lip?" she said, seriously enough to wipe the smile off Kev's face. We knew her well enough now to realise she could take a joke. But sometimes one of us would step too far over the line, and Anna would make sure we realised it, every single time.

Nige held up his hands to calm the situation.

"Look, we'll all do our bit. The Scout Group gets extra money for the new roof on the Scout Hut: we have a good time doing penny-for-the-guy: and if we win we get free fireworks, nosh and soda-pop... So, Steve, you go and fetch your Dad's flared trousers. I think I can scrounge an old pair of boots –"

"I have a wig we can use," Anna added.

Kev grinned. "The one you're wearing now, you mean?"

"I'll bring a Guy Fawkes mask," Anthony said.

"That just about sorts it. Meet back at HQ with all the stuff in an hour..."

* * *

"Your father was wondering if I could take the hems in a bit..."

Mum held up the pair of grey checked trousers for me to see. From the expression on her face, I didn't know if she wanted to laugh or cry. "He got married in these," she said, sort of wistfully, and her gaze drifted off to somewhere far away and long ago.

"Is that why he looks in pain on the wedding photos, Mum?"

"Don't be cheeky, Stephen. Your Dad was a very handsome young man, I'll have you know... And if he had a little more hair and a little less tummy, he'd look just as hunky today."

"I suppose you could always take that extra

material from the hem and stitch it into the waistband," I said with a smirk. Mum was hardly listening as she delved into the big cardboard box and pulled out the crinkly bright orange shirt I'd seen a few days ago, a rainbow-coloured tanktop, a purple neckerchief and a pair of strange-looking shoes with great thick heels and soles.

"They look like Frankenstein's boots," I pointed out. Even Mum had to chuckle at that.

"In those days," she told me, "if you had a pair of three-inch platforms, you were the bee's knees."

"You mean, cool?"

"I mean, red hot. When I first saw your Dad in these, I went all weak and wilting."

"What were you wearing at the time, Mum? Not a pair of those hot pants?"

She blushed, very faintly.

"Was it cool to wear hot pants back then, Mum?" I teased.

"Do you want these trousers or not?" she said snappishly, but still with a smile on her face, and with the slightest gleam of tears in her eyes for all those fond memories of so long ago.

* * *

"I think it suits you better than your real hair," Anna said, as Nige pulled on the black curly wig and waggled his head about.

"Yeah, yeah, man, wow, fab, groovy baby!" he sang, breaking into a psychedelic dance.

Neil exploded into fits of laughter, which went out of control into a bout of coughing.

I threw the flared trousers across and Nige dragged them on.

"What else have you got? I need a jacket or something..."

"Um, would you believe –" I held out the tank-top and Anna's eyes went wide.

"Wow, Steve, they're back in fashion now. You mustn't give that away."

"Well I'm not going to wear it. Do you want it?" I said. Anna's eyebrows lifted and she nodded enthusiastically.

The door opened and Anthony came in, wearing what was supposed to be a Guy Fawkes mask.

"It looks like Mr Hughes," Nige hooted. "I suppose it'll do. Now we have everything we need." He pulled a pair of worn boots from a plastic bag.

"Yes," said Anna, "but we've got to make the guy yet. We'll need straw and old papers to stuff it – and something to use for the head... And if you're serious about me having that tank-top, Steve, then we've still to find a jacket or something to hold all the stuffing in."

"This sounds too much like hard work!" Anthony plumped down onto one of the orange-boxes we used as furniture in the shed. "What could we use as a head – a swede or something?"

"We've still got the pumpkin we hollowed out for trick-or-treating..." Nige pointed to the shrivelling pumpkin head in the corner, its Halloween smile looking a little wrinkled now.

"It'll look stupid," Kev moaned. "It's too big for the mask, for one thing... And anyway, what's the point of going to all this trouble if we can't do well enough to win?"

"But we'll still get money from penny-for-the-guy," Anna said reasonably. "It'll all help towards the Scout Hut roof."

"Who cares about that?" Anthony glared back at her. "I want my free fireworks and hot-dogs."

"We all do," Nige interrupted, "but Anna's got a point as well. My own opinion is that if we, the Double Dare Gang, are going to get involved in this competition, then we mustn't let ourselves down with a half-hearted effort. So, there must be some way of making sure we have the best Guy Fawkes in the town – one that everybody will remember for years to come... Any ideas?"

I don't know quite where good ideas come from, but an absolutely brilliant one exploded in a burst of silent light inside my head just then. I didn't say anything right away, as I thought out the details to make sure that everything worked... Then Nige saw the excited, half-secret smile on my face.

"Well?" he said, knowing that look. "Spit it out, Steve."

I took a deep breath. "You might think it's crazy," I began, "but my idea is this..."

After I explained it, there was a long moment of silence, then Bri started up with that great bellowing laugh of his. Kev had a look almost of admiration in his eyes, and Anna was beaming broadly.

Nige nodded, chuckling quietly to himself. "Do you know, I think it's daft enough to work."

"Yeah," said Anthony, wishing he'd thought of it no doubt, "but who's going to do it? What about you, Steve? – I dare you..."

Nige stood up, so that his shadow, cast by candlelight, loomed inside the shed.

"Wait a minute, that's not fair. You can only make a dare when all of us can take part, and when we can double-dare you back... In this case, there's only one way for us to decide..."

Nige dug in his pocket and pulled out a dice.

"OK, Steve is one, Bri, you're two; Anthony – three, Kev – four, Neil – five. Anna and I will both be six, and if that number comes up we'll throw again between us. Agreed?"

We all nodded, and I felt that lovely tension come into the air; that special excitement that made me glad I was part of the best gang in the whole world.

Nige cupped the dice in his fist, brought it up to his mouth and blew on it, then rolled it out across the floor.

The dice rattled along the floorboards, hit the lip of the wooden doorstep and rolled back. We strained to see.

"It's a three!" Neil whooped.

We all looked over to the window, where Anthony was standing.

"Nice one, Ant," Nige grinned. "We won't tell anyone it's you. Honest."

* * *

It was one of those slightly misty evenings when the air seemed to smell of smoky metal. Above a thin, grey ground mist, a few bright stars gleamed faintly in the sky. Even though November Fifth was still two days away, somebody was letting off fireworks in one of the back gardens along the Wyland Park Road: we heard a rapid crackling, a bang; then a sizzling whoosh and a golden meteor trail, streaming upwards. The rocket popped with a crack into a glittering cascade that trickled sparks slowly back down the sky.

Neil took a good deep sniff.

"Ahhh! Smell that gunpowder..."

"No, I think its Anthony's wig," Nige said seriously.

We all glanced at the 'guy' jammed into the baby buggy. Its plastic facemask jiggled as Anthony spoke up angrily.

"I suppose you think this is funny!"

"You don't really look much different from normal," Anna told him, without a flicker of a smile. But Kev was grinning like the Cheshire Cat.

"Shall we try out the electronics, gang?"

"Aw, come off it – "Anthony started to struggle out of the buggy, and Bri pushed him back in with his big, square right hand.

"That's the whole secret of us winning the competition," Nige pointed out.

"You've got to do it, Anthony; otherwise you'll just be sitting there all night like, well, like a stuffed dummy..."

"Same as usual," I said. "Come on Nige, you've got the remote..."

Nige pulled the remote unit from his radio-controlled model car out of his jacket pocket and flipped on the power.

"Penny for the guy mister!" Nige said brightly to an imaginary pedestrian. "You won't see another one like this round the town. It sings, it dances, it tells fortunes – watch this!"

Nige manipulated the direction control on the remote while Anthony went all stiff and puppet-like and then began to do an odd jerky dance with his arms and upper body. Meanwhile, Kev, who was pushing the buggy, reached down and flipped on the red lights that were the mask's false eyes, and then the portable cassette recorder: a catchy little tune wafted into the cold night air. It had been a chart hit around the time that dinosaurs ruled the Earth. My Dad still loved it.

"Hey kids, that's not bad!" Neil said, pretending to

be the passer-by. "I haven't enjoyed myself so much since I was young, back in the 'Seventies... Here, take all the money I've got. It's only fifty quid, sorry, I wish I had more!"

He started dancing too – and then we all did, until we fell about in a fit of giggles.

"Well, what do you think?" Nige asked after we'd all calmed down. We wiped the tears from our eyes. Kev patted Anthony, who'd gone all floppy again, on the shoulder.

"That's brilliant. But, hey, Anthony, you've got to stay just like that until Nige works the remote. If you move or speak or anything, it'll spoil the illusion."

"I can't believe I'm doing this," Anthony grumbled from underneath his mask.

"It'll be worth it in the end." Nige licked his lips. "Just think of all those free hotdogs!"

* * *

We fetched our collecting pass from Mr Jesson at the Community College: the Scouts' bonfire party was held in the College's back field every year. From there it was a short walk across the footbridge to the supermarket car park, and then through to the shopping mall. Quite a lot of people were around, because the supermarket and the catalogue store were still open.

Kev turned on the recorder with the volume low. We all wore our best smiles as Anna held up the official pass and rattled the collecting tin. (We'd put some pennies in there already, so it sounded as though we were doing well for ourselves.)

"Penny for the guy, missus," Nige said as politely as he could to a lady leaving the supermarket with her trolley. "It sings, it dances... Watch."

He played with the remote and Anthony jigged about to the music, which Kev turned up louder. The woman smiled but hurried on with a slight shake of her head.

"Penny for the guy, sir – "

A man was striding by. He grinned when he saw us, nodded, and dropped a 5p into the tin.

"Yyyesss!" Nige pushed his fist into the air. "It works... I reckon first prize in Mr Jesson's competition is already ours!"

Actually, we did really well. After an hour in the mall, we tried our luck on the High Street. A couple of cafés, a late-night chemist, and several all-day pubs were open. The street was busy.

We turned the music up louder here, because of the noise from the traffic, which was moving slowly due to the road calming humps through the middle of the town. We could see the motorists smiling at us as Anthony went through his pantomime. Nige whispered something to Anna, who went to the edge of the pavement and held out the tin to the cars. A passenger wound down her window and dropped in some coins; then a couple more did the same. Then a lorry driver honked his horn as his juggernaut lumbered by; a taxi driver flashed his lights at us; a jogger stopped and said what a great idea he thought this was; a couple going to the theatre stopped and watched our show first, and put what looked like a pound into the tin. A group on their way to The Greyhound all tossed some money our way.

All in all, it was the best penny-for-the-guy we'd ever done.

"I've got to go home soon," Anna said about twenty minutes later. It was six-thirty and the town was quieter now. Also, the batteries in the cassette player had run down, so that all of the songs from the Seventies were playing at half speed. Not so much Glam as Gloom.

"I suppose we all have," Nige said. He was sniffing the air and looking distracted.

"Look, the chippy's open. Why don't we grab some chips, and then we'll walk you home, Anna. OK?"

"Why don't *you* walk me home, Nige?" she asked

coyly.

Nigel did a tomato.

"Because then I'd be a bigger dummy than Anthony. Anyway, Neil lives up your street, and Steve's house is on the way. It makes sense if we all go. Shall we count up our money first, though," he added, quickly changing the subject.

"Fifteen pounds and sixty-three pence!" Nige said with a mixture of surprise and satisfaction a couple of minutes later. He pushed the lid back on the collecting tin and carefully pressed the paper seal in place with his thumb.

We were standing huddled against the side wall of the fish and chip shop, out of the frosty cold. A plume of warm steam that smelt of cooking oil bloomed above us from the big extractor fan that breathed out the fumes from the shop. We were shivering now, all except Anthony, who was well huddled up in his outrageous gear and his wig and his mask.

"All right." Nige cupped his hands together and blew briskly through them. "Tell me what you want, give me your cash, and I'll go in and – "

"Wait a minute," Kev said. "We'll all go in. It's freezing out here, and we could do with a bit of a warm too."

"What about me?" Anthony piped up from behind his disguise.

"You can stay put." Nige readjusted the sign that said Penny for the Guy, hand-written on a scrap of cardboard with a black felt pen. He grinned. "Maybe you can earn enough money for us to pay for the chips!"

We piled inside and pretended to take our time choosing from the menu, so that we could get nice and warm before our chilly walk home.

In the end, we each had a bag of chips, and two pies to share. Bri also had a pickled gherkin, which was his favourite food (though it made him do some wicked big square farts). The chip-shop man scooped up some batter scraps for us as well, which were free.

"You look as though you could do with warming up," he said chattily.

Bri, with his mouth full of chips and gherkin, said something muffled in reply.

"We've been out collecting for the Scouts' bonfire party," Anna explained, noticing the party poster blu-tacked to the white-tiled wall.

The chip-shop man frowned. "You mean, that strange-looking guy in the baby buggy outside is yours?"

Nige nodded and half glanced around. And I saw his face fall as the chip-shop man added, "Then why are those kids running off with it?"

We scrambled out of the shop and ran to the edge of the pavement. The traffic lights had just turned green, and we had to wait for a string of cars to go by before we could give chase.

Whoever had stolen Anthony had a good start: by the time we reached the edge of The Square, which marked the centre of the town, the raiders had crossed the supermarket car park and were heading towards the footbridge over the river.

"I've got a really bad feeling about this," Nige said between gasps, as he struggled to get his breath back. Kev had run on a short way, but now trotted back to where we were gathered on this side of the car park. He was carrying the Penny for the Guy sign: it had been trampled, and was covered with boot prints.

"Did you see who it was?" Nige asked. Kev shrugged. "Well, I'm not sure, but..."

"It was Stonehead Henderson. I'll bet on it," Nige said. His face looked pale and tense. "Every year Henderson tries to ruin the Scouts' bonfire party. Do you remember a couple of years ago his gang actually tried to steal the bonfire? They worked half the night, carting wood and stuff from the College field to Henderson's garden... His mum made him take it back in the end, because she was scared the house would go up as well if he lit it... And then last year he tried to break into the Scout Hut and nick the fireworks... He's a real pain."

"So what's he playing at now?" Kev wanted to know. "He's a bit late to go collecting pennies for the guy..."

"I reckon he's taken Anthony for ransom. We only get him back if we hand over the money we've collected."

"Well, that's a mean trick," Anna said.

Nige shook his head slowly. "They don't come any meaner than Stonehead Henderson, believe me."

Henderson lived on the Wyland Park Road, down the bottom end near the Grove Hotel. Nige reckoned that once he and his gang were over the river, they'd cut down the side of the Community College's playing fields and head for home.

"Couldn't we take the money out of the tin and fill it with stones, or something?" Anna suggested.

Nige smiled at her. "Spoken like a true Double Darer... But I think Henderson would check before he handed Anthony over to us..."

"Wait a minute – " Kev had been scouting ahead, but now stopped. As we came up level with him he pointed at the ground. "They've turned off here, look."

Sure enough, the trail of the buggy and a scatter of footprints pressed into the dewy grass were clearly visible, leading away into the darkness. In the distance and off to the left, the white glow of floodlights from the College's all-weather pitch was blocked out by the building itself.

"They're not heading for the College, by the look of things..." Nige was squinting hard to follow the line of the trail. "The footprints go off to the right – "

"To the bottom field," I said.

"Where the bonfire is stacked," Anna said.

The awful truth hit us all simultaneously.

"I'd better go and phone for the police," Anna's voice sounded choked, "and the fire brigade as well... What will you do?"

"We've got to try and stop them. If Henderson sets light to the bonfire, it'll spoil the party for everyone."

We followed Nige's lead, and began running across the open field. We didn't go flat-out, partly to allow Neil and Brian to keep up with us; but also because we didn't want to arrive out of breath. If there was going to be a fight, we didn't want to be beaten before we started!

As we jogged together in a group, we began to hear shouts and laughter from up ahead. The towering pile of the bonfire started to loom out of the blackness, as our eyes adjusted to the gloom.

"They've gone round the other side," Kev said. Nige nodded grimly.

"So they can't be seen from the sports field or the College... I hope we reach them in time."

"Before they light the fire?"

"And before they duff up poor old Anthony, Steve. If they haven't done that already..."

We came up on Henderson's blind side, using the bonfire as cover. While we squatted low to the ground, Nige crept around just far enough to see what was going on. He came back a few seconds later.

"Henderson's brother, Clive, has got a box of matches. I think they're ready to start."

"Stupid idiots," Kev hissed. "Don't they know how dangerous that is!"

Neil said, "What about Anthony?"

"He's slumped in the buggy. I don't know whether they've really done him over, or what. But I think we'd better move now, before it's too late."

"What's the plan?" I asked. "Do we all hide behind Bri?"

Nige's smile flashed on and off.

"Bri will be useful, but we've all got to do our bit.

On my signal, Steve – you, Kev and Brian attack round that way: Neil and I will run round the other way."

Neil frowned.

"And then?"

"Your guess is as good as mine," Nige told him.

We took up our positions and waited nervously for a few seconds until Nige gave us the thumbs-up. Then we all broke into a run and started howling at the tops of our voices.

It was like a snapshot had been taken – flash / freezeframe. Henderson and all of his gang were standing there, frozen in surprise, with silly expressions on their faces.

Clive Henderson, who was our age, had an open box of matches in his hands. I leaped towards him and did my best karate kick, knocking the matches flying before he could light any of them. I yelled and said, "Hieeyaaa!" in my best Oriental accent, feeling a right prat a second later.

That broke the spell. A really nasty expression darkened Henderson's face. He bunched his fists and came at me. So did this other kid who looked like he should be haunting the Frankenstein Steps.

Neil came in from the side and crashed into the other kid, knocking him over and falling down on top of him, squashing him to the ground. Brian was busy fighting off three other boys who were climbing all over him, and Kev was doing some fancy kung-fu dancing around the group without getting too close to any of them.

I made ready to defend myself. Nige flew at Henderson, who grabbed his arms, swung him round and flipped him over the picket fence into the woodpile. Nige disappeared amidst a crackling of sticks and a small avalanche of boxes.

"You – are – history!" Henderson said as he squared up to me. He was bigger than I was, and was known to be one of the hardest kids in the town. I thought about what he'd said, and decided to believe him without arguing.

Even so, I wasn't about to turn around and run. I was one of the Double Dare Gang, and it was all for one and one for all.

So I clenched my fists and dared myself to face up to Henderson without trembling.

In the distance, I heard the shrill whoop-whoop of a police siren. It seemed to give Brian extra strength. With a roar he flung off the kids clinging on to him. Kev tried to kung-fu kick one of them, missed and fell to the ground with a thud.

Nige was struggling to free himself from the bonfire, and Neil had now got off the boy, who was pressed down into the mud.

Henderson realised he was beaten.

"I'll get my own back," he spat, glaring at me, and turned to run for it ...

That's when Anthony decided to come to life. He jerked like a robot that had just been switched on, rose slowly out of the buggy with his eyes glowing and came tottering towards Henderson, arms outstretched, going "Whoooooooooo!!!"

Henderson let out a thin squeal and stopped dead, giving me time to drop down on all fours behind him. Anthony pushed him flat in the chest, and Stonehead crashed over me onto his back, where he lay there kicking and screaming and crying for his Mam.

* * *

The police gave the Henderson gang a good telling-off for playing with matches and pinching our buggy. But that's about all they could do. Anthony was the hero of the hour, for keeping his cool and playing possum until the right moment; and Anna was the heroine, for calling the police just in time.

Mr Jesson and the First Kenniston Scout Group were delighted that we'd saved their bonfire. And because they were so grateful, we got our free entry to the party, and free hotdogs and coke.

But we didn't win the competition for the best

guy. The panel of judges didn't think that Anthony was realistic enough.

Mollie and the Great Removal Plan

Nobody had dared to do the Last Clap in assembly after Mr Hughes had given out the swimming certificates. All of us could see that he was not in a mood to Tolerate Any Nonsense. Outside, the rain was whipping against the huge glass windows of the hall: it was a wild and windy November Monday morning. But inside, everything was still and a bit tense, and not very nice.

It had been a long assembly with lots of notices. The bell for registration had already gone, and people were getting a bit restless. A few rows behind me, someone cleared his throat. Mr Hughes glanced up from his lectern and glared at him.

"Now finally, three further items. Firstly, our congratulations to Mr Jesson for organising such a successful bonfire party yesterday. I understand enough money was raised at the event to carry out the renovations to the Scout Hut – is that so, Mr Jesson?"

We all looked at Mr Jesson, who did a tomato and nodded without saying anything. It must be awful to be the centre of attention like that, I thought, even if you are a grownup.

"Well done, Mr Jesson," said Mr Hughes, "and to those of you who supported that particular good cause...

"Now, as I mentioned to you at the start of term, we are having workmen in school for the next couple of weeks. They will be redecorating the staffroom – and about time, no doubt – "Mr Hughes grinned briefly without seeming to enjoy it and looked at the back of the hall where most of the teachers were sitting. "And they will also be doing some repair work to the roof and tarmac at the side of the school, and in the side playground. This means that the area will be out of bounds until I say otherwise."

A faint groan went up from a number of kids, including me. That end of the school was out of the wind, and a lot of us used to gather there to stay warm in the cold weather, when it wasn't a wet break. The side playground was also a good place to play football and touch-tig, which we used to do most lunchtimes.

"Finally, as you know, Mr Dilks has been away from school since the start of the term with a, uh, a personal problem. I'm sorry that those of you in Mr Dilks' English classes have had your studies disrupted. However, I am pleased to say that we now have a teacher to take over from Mr Dilks until he is well enough to return..."

Mr Hughes half turned and indicated a rather thin

and dark-haired lady sitting at the end of the row on the stage, next to Mrs Carter the Year Seven Head. She sat like a statue, with her hands in her lap and her eyes staring straight ahead, not even looking at Mr Hughes when he spoke.

"We are pleased to welcome Miss Molloy to the school, and hope that she enjoys her time with us."

Mr Hughes's faint smile faded as he turned back towards us.

"Now, before I dismiss you, let me just say that it's likely to be a wet break today, which means you'll be in your tutor rooms – and I mean, in your tutor rooms! Not wandering about the corridors. Woe betide anyone I catch not in the right room this break time..."

"What does 'woe betide' mean?" Anthony asked Kev as we walked together along the crowded corridor towards our tutor rooms for a rushed registration.

Kev, who was supposed to know everything,

pushed his glasses higher up the bridge of his nose.

"It's an old Anglo-Saxon word," he explained. "Only teachers use it now. It means 'a week's detention, and a letter home to your mum'."

* * *

Kev and Anthony and I were in the same group for English, which we had first lesson that day. We decided on the way down that with a name like Molloy, we must call our new English teacher 'Mollie'. We saw her through the open door of the English stock room as we walked by. She was frantically searching for books or papers or something, and looked like she was going to take a couple of minutes at least.

A wicked grin spread over Kev's face.

"Come on, let's find seats together. She won't know Mr Dilks moved us apart..."

Because lots of the other kids were dawdling,

spending time in the loos or cloakrooms, we could take our pick. We chose two double desks at the far end of the classroom. They were against the radiator (nice and warm), and by the window that overlooked the side playground. As we settled ourselves, we saw a grubby-looking white van pull up and a couple of workmen in blue overalls pile out. They started unloading planks and ladders straight away.

I sighed. "It'll be ages before we can play touch-tig there again."

"It's going to be wet break anyway," Anthony moaned. "And we haven't got Mr Dilks to teach us... He was a good laugh, he was..."

"I wonder what his personal problem is?" I said, directing the comment at Kev.

"His wife, probably... I wonder what Mollie's going to be like..."

We found out soon afterwards. As we chatted, she swept into the room and dumped a set of class readers on the big teacher's table at the front.

"Right!" Her voice cracked like a whiplash. "You – " she pointed at Wayne Hardy who was sitting by the door. "Put that chewing gum in the bin! And you" – Karen Watson flinched as Mollie blazed at her – "stop your chattering now!"

Everyone shut up pretty quickly and faced the front.

Mollie's hard, glittering eyes moved slowly along the rows, pausing as she caught sight of Ray Vaughn secretly trying to finish off a tangerine.

"You, lad," she said, not yelling, but making her voice dangerously calm instead. "What are you doing?"

John Gilbert, Ray's best mate sitting next to him, spoke up. "Miss, it's his breakfast, miss..."

"I'm not talking to you. I'm talking to you, laddie. What's your name?"

"Miss, it's Ray, miss," Ray said, quickly spitting a pip

into his hand.

"Ray what?"

"Mond, miss," Ray answered, and giggling rippled around the room.

"I'm not amused," Mollie announced. She glanced with a sneer at Mr Dilks' untidy desktop. "Doesn't Mr Dilks have a seating plan?"

A few kids muttered that he didn't.

Mollie's face was red and glowing with her anger, and a vein stood out on her forehead. Her dark hair was brushed back and held in a bun, making her look older than she probably was. And her eyes were snapping with hostility.

"Seems like there are a number of things Mr Dilks doesn't have around here, including some discipline and good manners from his pupils. I can see I will need to make some changes... Now, back to you Ray-Mond... Why are you eating in class?"

"Miss," John Gilbert piped up. "He doesn't get a

breakfast at home. So we bring him biscuits or an apple - well, a tangerine today – and things, and – "

"Go and stand outside!" Mollie stormed, and when John just sat there looking shocked, she strode up to him and dragged him out by his lapel, slamming the door behind him with a boom that echoed through the school.

"I'll see you," she said to Ray, "at break. And now perhaps we can get on with some work..." Her voice moderated. "Our theme for the rest of this half term is 'point of view', and our first piece of creative work within that theme will be a parable, where I'll ask you to write in a way that explores someone else's point of view..."

I felt something sinking inside me like a stone, as Mollie picked two volunteers to give out the class readers.

"We're going to read extracts from this excellent horror-thriller book, Panic Station. You'll see that it's written in the third person – the 'he-or-she' voice.

Your task this lesson will be to select a scene and describe it from the point of view of one of the characters..."

Anthony blew out a big sigh as he unzipped his pencil case and pulled out a well-chewed biro.

"There's no doubt about it," he said, voicing our thoughts as well, "we'll have to do something radical about her."

* * *

"... and then she dragged Gilbo out of the room and slammed the door on him. At the end of the lesson, she sent him up to see Mrs Carter. Mrs Carter gave him a punishment essay to write, 'Why I must Not Answer Back to Teachers.' "

"At least that's not as bad as the titles Mr Hemphill gives, like 'A Day in the Life of a Teaspoon.' " Nige smiled at some bittersweet memory. Mr Hemphill was Nige's English teacher in Year Eight and although the two of them had their run-ins, Nige always said that

Old Hempy was OK really.

"But the whole point is that what happened to Gilbo wasn't fair!" Anthony's face was flushed with indignation. "And she had a go at Ray afterwards for eating in class – but it's true that he comes to school without breakfast, because his mum doesn't bother much. And he's always scrounging crisps and sweets off us, because he's hungry. We tried to tell Mollie this, but it's like she wouldn't believe us because we're kids... Why doesn't she trust us? Wasn't she a kid once?"

Nige shrugged, but Anna leaned forward and spoke quietly.

"Some people have a horrible time in childhood. Think about old Jethro in Nigel's story..."

"That was just a story," I blurted out.

"Then you've missed the point of it," Anna said.

Nigel glanced at her warmly.

"I think, from what you've said, maybe Mollie has

just come out of college. She's an NQT and she's been told not to be soft with kids – not to let them get away with anything."

"What's an En-Cutie?" Anthony wanted to know.

"Never mind," Nige said. "Trouble is, that's all she's doing. Before long, Steve, Tony, Kev, you'll be sitting there like good little boys, doing your work quietly and neatly. And you'll be absolutely bored stiff."

"I am already," Anthony announced.

"Do something about it, then," Nige replied, his eyes full of mischief. "Make life interesting..."

"But how?" Kev frowned, squinting through his mad-professor lenses.

Nige gave a huge sigh. "I thought you were a member of the Double Dare Gang? I thought you had become an expert in the art of playing great tricks on people? I thought you were the big-brain, Kev, who was never short of wild and crazy ideas!"

Kev looked mildly embarrassed.

"Well," he said slowly after a moment's reflective silence, "I suppose there's always Mr Lee's Joke Shop down the town..."

* * *

We reached the shop in plenty of time before it closed. The town centre was busy, with queues of rush-hour traffic waiting at the lights, their exhaust smoke blossoming in the air. Lots of people were hurrying home wrapped up in hats and coats and scarves, and the coffee shop on The Square was doing good business behind its steamed-up windows.

Mr Lee's was a tiny, tatty-looking shop down a side street just off the main thoroughfare. It was squashed between a newly-opened Balti house and a mobile phone showroom – 'Slash the Cost of Your Calls!!' a sign said in the window. The smartly dressed young man inside the shop glared at us when we pressed our mouths against the window and blew out so our cheeks ballooned and rippled. He mouthed something that made Nige laugh. When he got up from his desk and headed for the door, we legged it and piled into Mr Lee's...

Mr Lee had been around forever. My Dad said he used to come into the Joke Shop when he was a kid, like centuries ago. And Mr Lee seemed the same then as he did now, Dad reckoned. He was a long, thin man with a slight stoop – probably caused by his years of bending to avoid hitting the rubber bats and horror masks and vampire wigs that hung from the ceiling.

The shop had an odd smell, not nice but not nasty. A nostalgic smell. Sometimes when I went in there to buy or browse, I thought I could smell the sulphur stink of fart powder; sometimes the air was peppery; and sometimes sweetly quiet with the scent of make-up and cardboard boxes and plastic.

Not that it mattered; I just enjoyed going inside that magical domain.

Mr Lee smiled at us vaguely as we entered, as

though he was staring beyond the cluttered display cabinets and shelves, the walls themselves, and right through his customers, at something that none of us could see; into some other world where deeper jokes were being played. The pale blue eyes behind their thick-rimmed spectacles never focused quite right. He always seemed in a daydream.

"We're just browsing, Mr Lee," Nige said, "is that OK?"

Of course it was OK. Mr Lee never minded how long you spent in his shop, even if you didn't buy anything in the end. And it was because he was so pleasant that kids were friendly and respectful back to him; and only the worst kind, like Stonehead Henderson, would ever pinch anything or give him lip.

We had great fun trying on fake noses and moustaches. Neil tried to wear a werewolf mask without us seeing. The he spun round and went "RrrrAAArrr!" We yawned, but when he took the mask off we all screamed and pretended to dive for cover.

And we fell silent with our mouths open when Anna put on a long black lady-vampire wig, stuck her hands on her hips and fluttered her eyelashes at us. We all felt a little bit awkward then, and began busily searching through the racks of tricks and gags, and the novelties stuck to cards on the walls, pretending we weren't interested in girls.

In the end, after about half an hour, we plumped for some edible ink capsules, a whoopie cushion, a six-pack of stinkbombs, and a laugh-in-a-bag. Mr Lee smiled benignly as he added up the items. He pressed the switch in the laugh bag and a little chuckle began. Soon it became a belly laugh that none of us could resist. Within a minute we were all helpless, the tears streaming down our faces. Neil grabbed a false nose-and-moustache and put it on. That set us off even more, so that poor Kev nearly choked with all his laughing.

We didn't stop for ages, and even Mr Lee joined in, those pale blue eyes at last seeing something that was real. It all seemed very important somehow; as

the young man from the mobile phone shop next door put his lights out, locked up, and went home.

* * *

There are ways and there are ways of playing jokes, Nige explained back at the shed.

"For instance – " He held up an ink capsule between the pads of his forefinger and thumb. "How do you play a trick with this?"

"Stick it in someone's egg sandwich," Kev suggested at once.

Nige's eyebrows lifted. "Not bad. Except there's a risk the victim will feel the capsule in his mouth and spit it out before crunching it. And then the joke is spoiled."

"Drop it in someone's cup of tea," Anna said. "It says on the packet that the capsule dissolves. After a minute or two, the ink will be released into the tea and turn it a funny colour."

"Good. Except the capsule's too light to sink..."

"Hide it in a bag of jelly beans or other sweets and offer them round," was my idea.

"All right - except you might lose track of the capsule and it's taken by a friend, or even by yourself, and not the intended victim."

"All right then, smart alec," Neil grumbled, "what would you do to make the joke work?"

Nige told us.

And the plan seemed perfect.

* * *

By the next day the rain clouds had blown away. Anthony, Kev and I got to school really early. I told Mum I wanted to use the library to catch up on some late homework, but really it was so the three of us could sneak into Mollie's room and get all of our jokes ready.

We prepared the 'ink joke' just as Nige had

advised us, doing that first because it was the one that would get us into the most trouble if we were caught.

Then we took a few of the tiny stink bombs and put them under the legs of chairs: when people sat down the weight would crack the stink bomb casing and release the sulphurous pong.

We put the whoopie cushion under the real cushion on Mollie's chair, and we stuffed the laugh-in-a-bag down between the radiator and the wall, for use when the time was right.

Then we went and hung around at the back of the school until bell-time. (Couldn't play a good game of touch-tig or footie though, because the side playground was still out of bounds.)

We had picked today for two very good reasons. One was because every Tuesday there was Options Afternoon at the school. We called it Oh Ah Time. Instead of doing proper lessons, you could choose something really different, like Indian cookery or kit-making, orienteering or computer workshop. Because of Options Afternoon, the timetable was changed: there was no registration or assembly. Registers were taken from class lists in the first lesson, and sent to the office.

Secondly, our group's first lesson was English. The jokes we had prepared for Mollie would not have been disturbed by the time we arrived...

We waited around the entrance closest to Mollie's room, and when the bell rang we got in quickly, hurried over to the far side, and took our places by the radiator.

The rest of the class came in seconds later, followed by Mollie, who unlocked the walk-in store cupboard by the side of the blackboard, dumped her handbag beside her chair, and watched us settle with a hard and disdainful glare.

"Hey," Kev whispered urgently into my ear, "Some joker's nicked our laugh-in-a-bag... I just checked down the radiator, and it's gone!"

"You can't trust anyone round here," I said, but I was only half listening. My attention was focused mainly on the apple we'd placed on Mollie's table, with a little card that said 'For Miss Molloy. Sorry we've been a pain. From Class 7KY'.

"I can't smell the stinkbombs," Anthony said moments later. He was sniffing madly, his nose going like a rabbit's. "They should have gone off by now..."

That was true. All the kids in the class were seated. Only Mollie was standing, staring us down into scared and silent obedience.

Once you could hear a pin drop, Mollie slowly released the grip of her gaze and sat down in her teacher's chair.

Anthony gave a little whimper of anticipation. But there was no lovely wet farting sound from the whoopie cushion, and no glorious explosion of triumphant laughter either... Because Mollie had seen through our plans: she must have been on the lookout, watched us sneaking into her room, and then done a thorough search to remove the jokes we'd planned...

But surely she hadn't anticipated the secret of the apple? That trick had been planned by Nige himself. Nobody could have outguessed the apple joke. Could they?

"You've a lot to learn about the real world, children," Mollie said with a kind of sneer. She looked at all of the class as she spoke but particularly, I thought, at our side of the room.

Then she seemed to notice the apple for the first time. She read the note (in Kev's best joined-up but disguised handwriting), and smiled. It made her face look briefly human.

"Well, maybe I'm being a little too harsh... Our theme of work is 'point of view' after all..."

Mollie beamed at us. "Thank you, this is a very thoughtful gesture. And, as they say, one good turn deserves another... Ray-Mond, have you had any breakfast today?"

Ray looked shocked, as though he didn't know what to say to keep himself out of trouble. "Um, no, miss."

"Hasn't your friend – "

"John Gilbert, miss."

"Hasn't your friend John Gilbert given you anything?"

"Packet of crisps and a bubbly, miss."

"You aren't eating the bubble gum now, of course?"

Ray shook his head quickly. "No, miss. Miss, I put it in the bin, miss."

"All right, I believe you. Well, I hate the idea of your stomach rumbling all through my lesson. So here, have my apple, please. I'm sure your classmates won't mind..."

Mollie picked up the apple and held it out, encouraging Ray to come forward and take it. He walked hesitantly down between the rows of desks while we all looked on.

I heard Kev whispering beside me, "No, Ray, no."
But there was nothing we could do to stop it without
giving ourselves away.

Ray took the apple from Mollie.

"Go on," she said.

He bit into it, and ink sprayed out over his cheeks
and chin and filled his mouth with black.

Ray gagged and coughed and spat out the inky
mouthful. And although Mollie grinned at us through
her clenched teeth, nobody laughed.

Nobody at all.

* * *

Meanwhile, back at DDG HQ –

"This," Nige declared solemnly, "is getting serious."

"You're telling me," I said. "Not only did Mollie give
us extra homework for playing such a nasty trick on

Ray – she also kept us in at lunchtime and made us do grammar exercises."

"But we couldn't play football in the side playground anyway," Anthony added, as though that made some kind of difference.

We'd seen Nige on the way home from school that afternoon, and he'd ordered an emergency meeting of the Darers to discuss the vital business of The Mollie War and what we should do about it.

"Maybe we should just do nothing," Kev said, looking at us sheepishly, before leaping to his own defence. "I mean, she's not going to be here forever. Mr Hughes said she was just filling in while Mr Dilks got over his personal problem. Why don't we simply wait for her to go...?"

Anna and Neil were nodding in agreement with this, I noticed. But Nige's expression was troubled.

"That's not in the spirit of the Double Dare Gang," he said stoutly. "It's like being a yellow belly chicken – "

"Don't you think Kev's idea is just plain sensible?" Anna came back at him. "For once Nige, can't you see there's more of a choice than either doing something stupid, or being what you think is a coward?"

"Well – "

"Haven't you considered that Mollie may not be doing all of this out of spite? Perhaps she's really nervous about standing in front of you lot, trying to make the work interesting..."

"That's just the point," I grumbled. "It isn't interesting. It's awful, because you know you'll get a red line through your stories if Mollie thinks they aren't good enough... And she never laughs, Anna. She never seems to enjoy what she's doing – So how are we expected to enjoy it?"

I thought Anna would come in for the attack again, but she didn't. She became thoughtful too, as Nige had done. I glanced at Anthony and Kev, and then at Neil who wasn't bothering anyway because he was trying to blow a mega-bubble using a whole packet of bubblegum. The huge balloon expanded until you couldn't see his head. Then it quivered, before bursting softly to cover his face with a sticky white membrane.

"Right," Anna said firmly. "If you're so determined to make your point, then it's no good trying these silly schoolboy tricks on Mollie. She's obviously too clever for you anyway, and simply outplays you at your own game."

"That's put you in your place," Neil chuckled from behind the film of gum.

"So have you got a plan that would really let Mollie know what we think of her?" Nige wondered.

"As a matter of fact," Anna said, "I have."

"Let's hear it, then."

"Well, it's so good, I'm not going to tell you for free. I want a packet of Polos each from Steve, Anthony and Kev, a piece of bubbly from Neil, one of your custard creams, Bri... And I want a kiss from you,

Nige."

"Oh, no. No way – "

Nige started to do a tomato, but controlled it as he backed away, as though to hide himself behind Brian.

"Anyway, we don't even know if your wonderful plan is worth it. It might be naff."

"I know it isn't," Anna said. "And I'll tell you what: I'll reveal the plan to one of you – Steve, you'll do – if you promise not to pass it on. You can judge whether it's worth Polos and bubbly and a custard cream, and a big wet sloppy kiss from Nige."

"OK," I said, before Nige had a chance to disagree. All of the others began clapping and cheering. Bri did a shrill whistle that was so loud it made the window glass rattle.

"Come on then – "

Anna grabbed my hand and hauled me out of the shed. As she told me the plan, a slow grin spread over my face. But I felt very nervous as well as excited. It was a big plan – a daring plan – a plan truly worthy of the Double Dare Gang!

But would I have the guts to go through with it?

"It's worth it," I told the others when we came back in. "It's a brilliant plan. And if we can persuade enough of the class to do it, and if it goes smoothly, we shouldn't end up in too much trouble."

"No-one will be hurt," Anna added, "and I'm sure Mollie will get the point. Maybe she'll ask to take over another class, or something..."

"So," I chirped up, "get your bubbly out, Neil!"

"Oh," said Anna, "you can pay me the bubble gum and Polos and stuff later. But I'll take the kiss right now, Nige. OK?"

"Um – I'm not so sure I want – "

But there was nothing he could do about it. Neil and Bri darted forward and pinned Nige's arms behind his back. Kev dived for his legs to stop him kicking. And as Anna moved slowly towards him, loving every moment of it, Nige's face began to look as though he was about to swallow the biggest spoonful of medicine in the world.

* * *

The next day was as good as any. In fact it was better, because if we'd left it too much longer, I think all three of us would have yellow-belly-chickened out. We passed the word round at breaktime. There was some solid support, a few definite no's, and a lot of kids who said they'd think about it.

"It's not going to work," I said to Anthony and Kev as the bell went and we wandered back into school for third lesson. "There's not enough solid support. If only a few of us do it, we're going to look right prats!"

Kev shrugged. "Well we can try to drum up some more interest at dinnertime. But we must go through with it in English this afternoon, or forget about the whole idea. Now that we've actually told people, rumours will spread quickly: if the teachers find out, we'll be in deep doggie-do anyway!"

"Kev's right," Anthony agreed. "I say let's do it... In fact, let's dare ourselves to do it!"

"Anthony," I said, my tolerance at an end, "why don't you just go and bury yourself head first..."

More people seemed keen when we spoke to them at lunch. We said that we'd take the blame if Mollie and Mr Hughes took it all too seriously. And in any case, it was something that kids in school would talk about for years.

The riskiest part of the whole thing was sneaking into Mollie's room towards the end of lunch and hiding the piles of paper she kept in the storage drawers beside her desk. Then, when the lesson itself began, Kev and Anthony and I started talking loudly and laughing. Mollie swept in, unlocked her walk-in store cupboard, dumped her handbag beside her chair, and glared at everyone.

"Right! That's enough – stop your noise now!

Wayne, put that chewing gum in the bin – how many times must I tell you? AND STEPHEN AND KEVIN, STOP THAT ROW AT ONCE!"

We deliberately carried on talking. I glanced at Mollie with a big grin on my face, then glanced away again.

I think that's why she picked on me.

"I will not have you boys ignoring my instructions! Such bare-faced insolence!"

She had come right up to us and I was being dragged out of my seat.

"I'll see you both after school today – and Stephen," Mollie hissed very close to my ear, "how dare you ignore me. Get yourself down to the front desk, and that's where you'll stay for the rest of the term!"

So, it was to be me after all. Kev and Anthony and I had agreed that whoever got moved would do The Hard Part. One of the others would ask for the paper.

I took my bag and went to sit down at the front desk. This was always kept empty for naughty kids: it was right by the door – and a short walk away from Mr Hughes' office. I tolerated the eyes of the class on the back of my neck, as Mollie drew together the threads of the past few lessons, then said that she wanted us to begin a first draft of a story that explored someone else's point of view.

"Now you can either be the person whose point of view you're exploring, or you can be yourself, as it were. But in either case I want you to be sensitive to the way at least one other character in the story thinks, feels and behaves... Right, off you go. You have all of this lesson to work on your drafts, and because you'll be concentrating hard, I will expect absolutely no noise or talking at all!"

I got down to it after chewing my pencil for a few minutes...

We were just ordinary kids from an ordinary town. There was no reason at all why it should have happened to us in particular...'

Actually, I ended up quite enjoying myself, and thought it wouldn't be a bad life to be a writer. I was almost disappointed when Kev put up his hand and waited for Mollie to notice him.

"Yes, Kevin?" she said heavily, pausing in her marking.

"Please miss, my rough book's full. Can I have a new one?"

"You know it's your form tutor's job to give you a new book – "

"I'll carry on in my English book then, shall I, miss?"

"No, that's for your best work. This is only a draft of the story, remember... I'll let you have some scrap paper – but be careful not to lose it. Come out and fetch it then!" she snapped.

"OK, miss."

Kev sauntered cheerfully down to the front while Mollie pulled open one of her storage drawers, then another, with growing impatience.

"I thought I'd restocked these last Friday," I heard her muttering. Kev was standing there holding his hand out, trying not to smirk.

"There's some paper in the stock cupboard, Kevin – " Mollie said, and the shock jolted through me like lightning.

"Oh, no, don't bother. I'll fetch it myself. I don't want you messing things up in there..."

The relief felt like a warm bath – only to be followed by nervousness as my heartbeat started to race and my stomach began to churn. It was like leaping the garage roofs all over again!

Mollie stood up and pushed back her chair. She strode towards the stock cupboard. Daring instant punishment, Kev was already picking up the bunch of keys from her table. "Green key," he mouthed without speaking, as Mollie disappeared inside.

This was the moment. I slipped out of my chair, caught the keys on the run as Kev pitched them to me, quickly found the key with the green tab, and swung the stock cupboard door closed.

Just for an instant, as the light inside there changed and Mollie began to turn, I saw the disbelief and outrage on her face.

Then I'd slammed the door shut and turned the key.

"Right, everybody out!" Kev yelled.

Our one hope was that there wouldn't be pandemonium. What we didn't want was to be remembered as just another bunch of kids going out of control.

I opened the classroom door and was pleased to see that people were picking up chairs, desks, piles of books, pot plants off the windowsill – and began walking out quietly with them, as though they were doing an errand.

That was good, because it meant we had a fair chance of completely stripping the classroom without being suspected.

Anthony ran to the back of the room and pushed open the fire door. The workmen were still out at lunch, so more kids began leaving that way.

Meanwhile, Mollie had started banging on the storeroom door and shouting in her severest and most menacing voice for someone to let her out.

Kev grabbed a couple of chairs. Anthony carried as many textbooks as he could manage. I hefted up a desk, and away we went towards the playing fields.

Just before I left the room, Mollie's shouting subsided to a very ominous silence...

"Teachers will spot us here," Kevin panted as he struggled with his chair. "It was a bad move to come out through the fire door."

"We'll be in for it anyway," I pointed out, straining to keep up with them as I shifted the weight of the desk in my arms to ease my aching back.

"You're not kidding – look!"

Anthony's expression was a mask of fear. We turned and saw Mollie storming out after us. Some yellow-belly chicken must have released her! She looked totally berserk.

Anthony dropped his armful of textbooks, and being the fastest runner in the school, and me being a few desperate steps behind him, we got quite a long way away by the time Mollie reached us.

Behind her, I saw dozens of kids' faces watching from the windows of the classrooms. I wondered what my Mum and Dad were going to say about all of this, and I wondered what terrible punishment Mr Hughes was going to inflict. And I wondered –

"Come here, you little thugs!"

Mollie made a sort of swipe and grab for Kev. He ducked back and spun out of the way. In her rage, Mollie instantly turned on me. She lashed out, missed, then stepped in towards me and pushed me hard.

I stumbled backwards and lost control of the weight of the desk. It dropped and I crashed into it, scraping my shin on one of the legs.

Mollie took advantage of it and snatched at my shirt. I was lying on my back and she was looming over me, darkly furious.

But her voice was quiet and as tight as a guitar string as she spoke.

"I'm going to make sure you never forget what you did!" she hissed. "What a stupid, pointless, childish, vindictive thing to do... Why can't people like you just grow up!"

"Because," I said back, like a door opening out of the pain and the fear of what was probably going to happen, "we don't want to turn into people like you..."

"I'll get you excluded!"

Now who's being childish, I thought.

"You hurt me when you pushed me over just now. Kev's my witness..."

Her eyes became shocked and confused, and I

think, just then, she began to see things from our point of view.

"But miss," I added, "to save us all a lot of trouble, I think we could do a deal..."

* * *

I never expected her to agree. But she did. Mollie didn't take the matter further, and I didn't make any fuss about my bruised shin.

We all got a good telling off from Mr Hughes – even the girl who'd let Mollie out of the stock cupboard – but letters didn't go to our parents, since Mollie said she'd rather let the whole matter rest.

It rested uneasily, but not unpleasantly, for the next five weeks until the end of the term, when we heard that Mr Dilks was coming back. It seemed he had got over his personal problem and would be returning at the start of the new term.

In our Year Seven Christmas Assembly, on Mollie's last-but-one day at the school, Mr Hughes made one of his l-o-n-g speeches. He thanked Mollie for the valuable contribution she'd made, and wished her well in her teaching career.

Afterwards we were invited to show our appreciation "in the usual way", and all the Year Sevens applauded loudly.

Nobody did the Last Clap.

And nobody ever found out where the laugh-in-the-bag was coming from.

The Gift

We were just ordinary kids from an ordinary town. There was no reason at all why it should have happened to us in particular.

It was December 17th, almost at the end of that long dark dreary tunnel between Guy Fawkes' Night and the start of the Christmas holidays. In less than a week the term would be over and we could forget all about work and Mr Hughes and Mollie and the rest of it – just looking forward to a fortnight of videos and books and sweets and good films on TV (maybe). And presents, of course.

Mrs Carter had already done a Year assembly all about the True Spirit of Christmas. She told us that the festive season was not just about having a good time; stuffing yourself full of food and drink, and feeling pleased if you had a bigger or better present than your friend.

"The True Spirit of Christmas," Mrs Carter said, "is all to do with giving; with kindness, with the care and thoughtfulness that one person shows to another. Christmas has nothing really to do with possessions at all, with wanting or having things. At its heart lie the ordinary human qualities of love and selflessness... Just remember that, won't you, and give some thought to those people less fortunate than yourselves..."

Amazingly, a lot of kids in the hall started to applaud. I joined in, and so did Anthony and Kev, though none of us did the Last Clap, because we kind of saw the sense of what she'd said.

Then, in Tutor Period, we had to write a letter to Santa Claus. This was different from the True Spirit of

Christmas, I thought, because it was all about wanting things. After what Mrs Carter told us, I almost felt guilty telling Santa that I'd like a Playstation Two, please, and a couple of really good games to play on it; and a pair of AirWear trainers; and, if it wasn't too much trouble, a new Action Guy Special Forces Survival Kit water canteen, to replace the one that had exploded when I'd tried to jump the garage roofs... Except I wasn't sure you could get the water canteen by itself, and in any case I didn't really believe in Santa Claus any more.

Even so I added – 'And it would be really kind of you, Santa, if you could let it snow over Christmas. Or even better, this afternoon, or at least by tomorrow. It's just that playing out is more fun in the snow, and it's not like you'd have to spend any money or anything. Hope you get all your wrapping done by Christmas Eve. Give my regards to the reindeer. Best wishes, Steve Bowkett. PS: I'll get Mum and Dad to leave the mince pie and glass of sherry in the usual place (you must be really fed up with mince pies by now, and you must be permanently bladdered on the sherry!).'

I addressed the envelope to Santa Claus Esquire, Santa's Grotto, North Pole, The Arctic, Northern Hemisphere, The Earth, The Solar System, The Galaxy, The Local Cluster, The Universe, Infinity, Back of Beyond, LE17 9HF.

Then I drew a stamp with the Queen's head on it, added a crown and a little moustache and handed the work in as the bell for next lesson started ringing.

* * *

We'd all arranged to meet on the walkway by the park, at the highest part of the embankment. The day had been bright but freezing cold, and frost was already forming on the ground again, even though the sun had just gone down behind the houses. Where the sunlight had not reached – like the north-facing side of the bank – the frost stayed all day. And that's where we were going to play our game of sledging.

Nige was already there when I arrived. He'd started our sled-run by sliding down a few times on a big square of cardboard box, folded over and turned up at the front..

"Mum had a new washing machine," he explained. "It was an early Christmas present."

I rattled out a little rhythm on the tin tray that I'd brought. "I haven't tried this out, but I hope it'll work."

We waited for a while until the others arrived. Nige started jumping up and down, flapping his arms around himself to keep warm. I stood away from him and stared at the sky...

It was orange through the trees, turning to green and then purple as you went higher. The church spire stuck up like a dark icicle. Further round, hanging low over the nearby roofs, the moon and a really bright star were stamped on the heavens, very close together. In another half an hour or so, all of the stars would be out and it would probably be too dark to bother. I wished the others would hurry up...

A loud belch echoed across the park.

"Anthony's here," Nige said with a silly twisted grin. A belch was Anthony's trumpet call and his speciality. Once he did it so loudly in the playground that Mr Hughes had heard him from his office. Gemma Freed told on him, and Anthony had to stand in the corridor outside the Head's office all that afternoon for being rude.

He came trotting across the park, leaving a trail of dark footprints in the just-frost on the grass. As he reached the bottom of the bank, he whirled his round plastic tray up at us like a giant Frisbee: it sailed close over our heads and vanished into a patch of bramble on the other side.

"Missed us both – useless shot!" Nige called.

Anthony burped again and scrambled past us to retrieve the tray.

We spotted Kev almost immediately afterwards. He was walking at a more leisurely rate, pulling what looked like a proper sledge behind him. And so it turned out to be.

"Dad made it," Kev declared with some pride. He turned the thing round so we could examine its strength and sturdiness, the padded seat, and the finely fashioned runners that had been waxed with the same stuff his Dad used to wax the family's skis, Kev told us.

Nige looked pig-sick with envy for a few moments, until Kev said that we could all have a go on it.

A minute later, Neil shrill-whistled over to us as he reached the end of Auriga Road. Bri was beside him, carrying one of those silvery helium-filled balloons you get at the funfair.

"Late night shopping down the town," Neil explained. "There was a balloon man giving them out in the mall... We both got one, but I let mine go to see if people would think it was a UFO."

"Whatcha going to do with yours, Bri?" I wondered. Beside me, Nige chuckled.

"I shouldn't hang on to it for too long, it'll carry you up in the sky."

"Yeah?" Brian glanced suspiciously at his balloon that showed our twisted reflections as it tugged and swayed on its string. After giving it some thought, he went over and tied it carefully to a nearby tree.

Anna joined us soon afterwards, trudging up the bank with a piece of heavy sacking to slide on.

And so we were ready to begin.

There were no rules to follow, except not to crash into anyone's back. Although Nige had made the run, we let Kev open it officially on his posh hand-made sled. Nige had picked a good spot where the bank was really steep, but there was a bush at the bottom, wild lilac, so you had to jink sideways to avoid it and come skimming out safely on to the flat grass of the Park.

We had bursts of mad sledging, getting in as many goes as we could while the light lasted. The air trembled brittly with our screams and shrieks: but it was hard work and soon we'd laughed and joked and sledged ourselves to exhaustion.

Neil quit first, standing at the bottom of the bank, stooped over with his hands propped on his knees, panting like a racehorse. Big plumes of steamy breath rose around him.

"I'm knackered," he declared.

Bri dived on his surfboard-like rectangle of plastic sheeting and skimmed down the bank like a big square torpedo, deliberately sideswiping Neil and knocking him right off his feet. Neil dropped like a felled tree. But Bri, out of control himself, hit a tuft of grass which spun him sideways and tipped the sled over: he went tumbling in a spray of frost-smoke with his arms and legs flailing.

"You big dumb blob!" Neil yelled, picking himself up and wiping the icing-sugar crystals off his coat and out of his hair. "You did that on purpose!"

Bri didn't deny it, but just came lumbering over with a big square grin on his face. He shrugged, happy to accept whatever trouble Neil was going to make for him.

Neil never really got into much of a temper, not a real blazing one. But what Bri did had annoyed him, and he actually stormed up to Bri and jabbed him in the chest.

"That wasn't funny. That hurt me, Bri, and you'd better say you're sorry, or..."

Neil's common sense stopped him there. You couldn't threaten Bri – or at least, you couldn't carry out the threat, because Bri was one of the biggest kids in the school. He was as tough as bricks and had never been known to run away from anyone. Even Stonehead Henderson was scared of him deep down, which was why he hadn't bothered us after we'd foiled his plan to set light to the Scout Group's bonfire.

"Why'd you do it, Bri?" Neil demanded to know.

"Just thought it would be a laugh, that's all."

"Well I'm not laughing," Neil ranted. "It was a

brainless thing to do – because you're brainless, that's why! Brainless Bri they ought to call you!"

"That's enough. Break it up."

Nige came between the two of them like David between two Goliaths and pushed Neil back.

"Nobody's perfect," Bri said quietly. We'd heard people say that to him before, as though they were telling him it wasn't his fault he didn't have much going on between his ears.

"Too right," Neil said fiercely, "especially you!"

"Don't spoil it, Neil." Anna walked over to where the rest of us were gathered. Her hair was tied back in a ponytail tonight, and she had on blue ear-muffs and scarf and gloves, and a red quilted jacket. Thing was about Anna, she never had to shout for people to listen.

"This is such good fun, just being here with you guys, it would be awful to quarrel. Come on you two, shake hands and be friends."

"Dunno about that." Neil folded his arms and looked stubborn.

"Oh, just do it, Neil," Nige said impatiently. "The light's nearly gone. We don't have long before we've got to go in."

"Well..." Neil looked at the ground and then at his hand, which he held out to Bri. Brian's massive square hand folded right over Neil's, and he shook it, grinning, happy the row had been avoided.

"Who's that?"

Kev's question cut through the moment. He pointed as we looked out across the dark open space of the Rec.

A kid was standing there, about thirty feet away, like a white smudge made out of the pale frost itself.

"I don't know him," Nige decided. "Do any of you?"

There was a general shaking of heads. I was pretty sure he didn't go to our school, though I couldn't guess which other one it could be: he looked about my age, and there was no other middle school in the town.

"Maybe he's from the travellers' camp up the road," I said, thinking aloud.

"What do you want?" Neil grumped, still feeling hostile perhaps from his brush with Bri. And I suppose we all felt a bit possessive about our playing-place.

The strange, thin boy just looked back at us and the seconds passed by, and the sky grew a little darker.

It was clear this kid wasn't going to speak, or even shift come to that. He was probably frightened, I thought; because he was bone-thin and quite short, a real wimpy sort of kid. He had straight hair, long and scruffy and bleached yellow as corn, and a tatty jacket and frayed jeans with holes in them.

"My friend asked you what you wanted!" Anthony said loudly in that gruff way he thinks makes for tough street-speak.

The boy shrugged. He reminded me of one of the urchins you find in Charles Dickens stories. Maybe he'd come to beg money. Or maybe he was just lost.

Anna, being Anna, took pity on him while we stood about trying to look casual. Bri was playing with the breath that came steaming out of his mouth; making big clouds of it, then trying to blow smoke rings.

I wondered why I couldn't see the new boy's breath, as Anna went across and took him by the elbow and brought him over to join us.

"My name's Anna," she said with one of her brightest smiles. "And this is Nige, Neil, Steve, Bri, Kev and Anthony. We call ourselves the Double Dare Gang – but we're OK really, honest... What's your name?"

He glanced at each of us, then at Anna, with a kind of kicked-puppy sadness in his eyes. "It's Christopher," he said at last. And he smiled as though he'd accepted us here on this quiet embankment

113

under the cold December sky.

"I just thought the game you were playing looked like good fun... And I thought maybe you'd let me join in – "

"We haven't got a sled to lend you," Neil interrupted grumpily. "There's seven of us, and seven sleds. So, sorry and all that."

"Don't be so mean," I said. "Here, you can borrow mine for ten minutes. I'm bushed anyway."

Chris took my tin tray gratefully. And to cement our friendship, I dragged my bag of mint imperials out of my coat pocket and offered him one – then had to offer them round to everyone, of course. Odd though, but when I'd done that there seemed to be just as many in the bag. If not more...

"Well – thanks." Chris beamed, and then he was off, leaping aboard the tin-tray-sled, whizzing down, tumbling in a bundle at the bottom; scrambling back up and zooming down again without pause, trailing laughter. He played as though he meant it, as though the whole world and its winter had been made just for him to enjoy himself tonight. As though nothing else mattered.

"He's a pinbrain," Neil declared, with a sneer that was as sharp and cruel as knives.

"He's just having a good time." Anna smiled at Neil, then the smile widened as she glanced back at Christopher. "Seize the moment."

Which is what it said on the plaque above the entrance to our school.

Chris played himself out after ten minutes, and then staggered back to us, dragging his scuffed shoes across the battered grass at the bottom of the embankment. The soles flapped like dogs' tongues. His socks were grey and threadbare.

"Oh, that was brilliant! That was great!"

He was panting and hardly able to gasp out the words. But his eyes glittered like stars, and with a light that was finer and farther away.

"Thanks lads... Thanks Anna... Thanks..."

"Don't mention it," I said, and offered another round of mint imperials.

Chris shook his head and held his hands up as he brought his breathing under control. "Look, you've been really kind, and I want to give you something in return... What would you like?"

We all gazed at him, then at each other; kind of embarrassed because we could all see he had nothing but what he stood up in.

"Well," Neil said, still holding on to his bad temper. "That's a really nice pair of shoes you've got there. And hey, that nifty shirt!"

"Cut it out, Neil!" Anna snapped, hating his heartless teasing. But Chris just smiled faintly, as though all of this was above his understanding. Or beneath his contempt.

"Chocolate would be nice," Brian added without thinking. "You got any chocolate, Chris?"

Anna and I started to explain to Brian, but Chris cut through our careful explanations.

"Sure."

And then he did something I'll never understand and that I'm not even sure I believe even now.

Chris opened his hand and there was chocolate – a family-size Cadbury's bar, which he held out to Neil, whose mouth gaped open as if to start eating.

The trick was done beautifully, suddenly; a turn of magic so smooth that none of us could figure what had happened.

We stood like shadowy cardboard cutouts in the dark, hardly daring to look at each other's faces and give away the stupid expression on our own.

"That was pretty neat..." Kev took the chocolate from Chris, broke it open, peeled off the paper and purple tinfoil, and munched off a chunky corner. He shook his head, as if realising only now that he'd not been having an hallucination.

"What else can you do?" Nige asked cautiously, perhaps thinking of two-ton bags of pick'n'mix and swimming-pools full of foaming cola.

"Whatever you like." Chris said it too casually to be kidding us.

"Such as?" came Nige's challenge, a kind of ultimate dare – because if it was only a trick after all, then the world would have changed back to what most people believed it to be.

But part of me wanted to say no. A bit of trickery I could cope with – Chris could have pulled the chocolate from his jacket by sleight of hand. He'd been to Mr Lee's, of course. It wasn't proof of anything. Yet, if he did prove it... If he did...

"Gimme a Christmas tree." Nige grinned wickedly. "With plenty of lights flashing on and off, and a pile of pressies all around... Go on, man – go for it!"

"No!" I said aloud, and too late.

The air nearby was already changing, and a wash of coloured light was brightening on Chris's forehead and cheeks. Kev was facing the same way, and so I saw the tree appear as two tiny miniatures reflected in the lenses of his spectacles – a twinkle of rainbow gleams and glints of tinsel-wrapped shapes.

I turned around feeling stunned, and there it was. The proof.

The Christmas tree was about six feet tall and richly decorated with baubles and lights which, as Nigel had wanted, flickered on and off, sometimes slowly and sometimes almost too fast to follow. An untidy jumble of presents lay scattered around the base.

"I think," Kev said in a small voice, "I'd better fetch my Dad..."

We hardly noticed him disappearing into the darkness. Nige had taken the initiative and walked over to the tree, with the rest of us following as though aliens from outer space had just landed, and we were the first human beings they'd met.

"How did he do that?" Neil wondered, touching

one of the flashing lights to make sure he wasn't dreaming. He didn't ask Chris directly, of course; though we were all sure he could make as many of them as we liked...

Anna was laughing quietly, sort of to herself – but her eyes were wet and bright, and the laughing sounded a bit like crying as she went up to Chris and gave him a hug.

"Thanks, Chris. That's wonderful. It's the best Christmas present you could have made."

"Don't know about that," Neil said, eyeing the pile of colourful boxes by the tree.

A few minutes later we saw the flare of a flashlight away up on the embankment, and Kev's silhouette and a couple of larger shadows beside him.

"What do we do now, Nige?" I asked. But for once it seemed Nige was lost for ideas, as Kev and his father and Mr O'Connor, who was a policeman in the town, came scuffling down towards us.

Chris's face was pastelled in the soft colours of

the Christmas tree as Mr O'Connor grabbed him by his jacket collar and shouted at him – "What the hell do you think you're playing at!"

I thought I saw Anna wipe away some tears, and Neil made himself busy gathering up his sled and saying, well, he reckoned he ought to be getting back home now...

Mr O'Connor was dragging Chris away and Mr Howells was speaking sharply at Kev, accusing him of getting mixed up in stuff that could be dangerous. He shook Kev like a little boy who'd been naughty, then pushed him out of the way and stalked up to the tree, which he kicked over and started tramping on it.

"No!" I yelled, and it was echoed by Nige who flung himself on top of Kev's father like a terrier and tried to force him over.

With a snarl, Mr Howells flung Nige easily aside. I looked at Bri and nodded to him – and we both started moving to help Nige out.

But then Anna's voice cut through the air, a sharp scream of despair.

"No!"

We turned and saw Mr O'Connor dragging Chris along like a sack of potatoes, up the bank towards the back gardens beyond. And Chris wasn't doing anything to stop him, as though his miracles were not to be trusted now and the spell of the night had been broken.

"Right behind you, Chris!" I yelled, and started running with the others, as Mr Howells finished trampling down the Christmas tree, struck a match and set fire to it.

* * *

Things happened fast after that. We went to Kev's house where, amazingly, we were let in and told to sit down and shut up. Four of us: me, Nige, Bri and Anthony, were squashed up on the couch. Anna and Neil shared one armchair, while Chris was pushed into the other. Kev stood by the window with his father beside him. Mr Howells' expression was strained, and the skin looked tight around his mouth.

Not more than a few minutes later, the doorbell rang and other grown-ups came in on a wave of cold air, the Reverend Bright, and Mr Bailey who was chairman of the town's Chamber of Trade and Commerce. Kev's Mum fluttered about asking these important people if they wanted tea or coffee, or perhaps a small glass of sherry. Mr Howells told her not to be so damned silly, and to stand out of the way.

Mr Bailey spoke a few brief words to Kev's father, and then the Reverend Bright went and stood in front of Chris, looking down at the top of his bowed blonde head.

"Now, Christopher," said the priest in a way that was meant to sound kindly, "I've heard what's been happening over at the embankment, and now I want to hear it from you... But you've got to think very carefully about all of this, because lies are not going to help anybody. That's right, isn't it, Christopher?"

Chris looked up and his eyes were filled with an innocent light. He nodded, and told the Reverend what had happened in a simple and honest way.

"That's just how it was," Nige confirmed.

The Reverend ignored him, and continued to ask Chris lots of questions that went on and on, as though Chris was bound to change his story in the end under the pressure of common sense.

Quite soon Mr Hughes the headmaster arrived, and Mrs Porter-Smith, who was the Lady Mayor of the town.

There were more and more questions, about where Chris had come from and who his parents were, and who had helped him to do the trick with the Christmas tree... Most of them Chris couldn't answer, or didn't want to. Mr Hughes took this as insolence and started to lose his temper like he did at school.

"Wait a minute!" Mrs Porter-Smith's commanding

voice cut through the hubbub.

"Shouting at the boy isn't helping. Let's try things a different way, shall we?"

Then there was a long silence, and the air kind of tightened up in that crowded room. I knew what was coming. I think we all did, deep down in the secret places of our hearts.

"Now, Christopher," Mrs Porter-Smith said sweetly. "It's not that we disbelieve you... But you've got to admit that what you and these other children have told us is, well, rather unusual. So, we are going to need a little proof, aren't we – because this is very, very important..."

"Whatever you like," Chris agreed cheerfully. And the little smile went out of the woman's face and she stood up straight, looking quite shocked.

"Perhaps something small, to begin with." Reverend Bailey stepped over with his hands clasped in front of him. "Just so we can really be sure you're telling the real truth."

Chris opened his right hand and a rosebud lay in his palm: opened his left hand and a butterfly flew away: his right hand again, and there was a gold pocket-watch: left hand, and a fancy ring just like the one the vicar was wearing.

"Good – God – " the Reverend breathed the words and made the sign of the cross.

"Something more," said Mr Bailey. "What else can you do?"

Chris grinned at him. "Whatever you like!"

His hands opened and closed and gifts spilled from them like rain; coins and jewels, meaningless bits of plastic, things we couldn't identify, pieces of electrical circuitry, sweets and stones, eggs and living creatures, counters and dice, treasures and worthless toys. It was all the same to Christopher.

"More," Mr Hughes was almost dancing with excitement, while Mrs Porter-Smith's mouth had grown wet with greed.

"More, child, more..."

A larger object came into view, a stain in the air at eye height between Christopher and me. It was moving slowly, and its skin was reddish and not quite fully fashioned. Mr O'Connor, who'd been a cop for twenty years, gave a groan as the monster dropped to the carpet with a thud and just lay there, twisting, not this thing nor that; neither here nor there – just a sad mixture of all these adults' dark and bloody dreams.

Chris looked as though he was lost in a fever of giving, and I couldn't tell what he was feeling just then.

"We've got to stop this," I whispered to Nige, who was squashed up right beside me. He looked from me to Chris and back to me again, and seemed unsure for once.

"Can't you see what they're doing to him? We must end it, Nige... I dare you."

That jolted him properly awake. His face looked fierce and determined suddenly.

"And Steve, I double-dare you! After three – one –two - three!"

With a yell, we jumped up, startling everyone. Nige grabbed a cushion and flung it at the standard lamp in the corner. The lamp crashed over and the room went dark.

I found Chris's arm, took hold and hauled him up. Mrs Porter-Smith was shrieking for us to stop – stop! and Mr Hughes was shouting like he did in his worst temper at school.

There were too many people between us and the door. I searched madly around for a way out.

"Patio doors," Anna said breathlessly. She pointed to the long curtains behind us and we ran towards them.

Mr O'Connor's voice cracked out a threat. He lunged after us, but Bri stood in front of him like a wall, and even Mr O'Connor hesitated to push by.

I dragged aside the curtains, fiddled with the handle, and shoved the doors open wide.

Then we were out in the night, hurtling across Kev's lawn to the hedge at the bottom of the garden. We scrambled through, not caring that we scratched ourselves and tore our clothes; ran up the embankment and down the other side...

Nige and Anthony had kept up with us. Kev on pain of being grounded had stayed where he was; Neil and Bri had probably gone the back-garden way to their homes.

The five of us, me, Chris, Anna, Anthony and Nige, ran along the embankment until it downsloped to bring us out at the corner of the Park. It was full night now. The sky was crammed with stars, and a faint freezing mist hung in the air around us, and lay draped in the bare branches of the trees.

"We got away from them," I said happily, through teeth chattery with the cold.

"Good on us," Nige agreed, "and tough luck on them... But it's late now. I guess we'd better be getting back."

"What about you, Chris?" Anna wondered. "Where will you go?"

"Oh." He shrugged. "I've got a home to go to. Don't worry about me."

"Shall we walk with you there?"

"No need, it's not far away."

Behind the shadow, I thought softly. Beneath the stone. Within the wood.

We had all stopped now we'd reached the avenue of trees, limes and chestnuts, that bordered the path on this edge of the Park.

"Well, so long," Chris said as he moved off into the darkness. He turned once to give us a little wave.

"So long."

We watched him dwindle and fade like a faint pencil sketch on the misty paper of the night; becoming a blur, a memory, and then nothing at all.

"I suppose," Nige said, "I'll see you all at school tomorrow... Er, um – " He gave an awkward little cough. "Shall I walk you home, Anna?"

"Great, thanks," Anna said. I didn't see if Nige had done a tomato or not.

So we went our own ways. It was quite late, and I supposed I would be in trouble over it... Or maybe not, I thought. Perhaps on a night like this it wouldn't occur to Mum and Dad to tell me off. Maybe they too would be touched by the spirit of Christmastime.

And you know, although the sky had been clear as we'd run along the embankment, by the time I turned into Auriga Road clouds had drifted over and it had gently started to snow.

About the Author

Iwas born and raised in the mining valleys of
South Wales. My favourite place to play was out
on the hills where my imagination had plenty of
space to expand.

When I was ten I joined the Double Dare Gang. We
used to dare each other to do things, but the one
who made up the dare was double dared, so we all
had to do the dare. If you didn't you were a yellow-
belly chicken. And if that happened more than three
times you were thrown out of the gang!

My family moved out of Wales when I was thirteen.
I went to a new school where one of my subjects
was French. Because I had never learned any
French, my teacher made me sit in the naughty
corner and 'get on with something constructive'.
That's when I started to write, just for myself, and